# All Kinds of Family

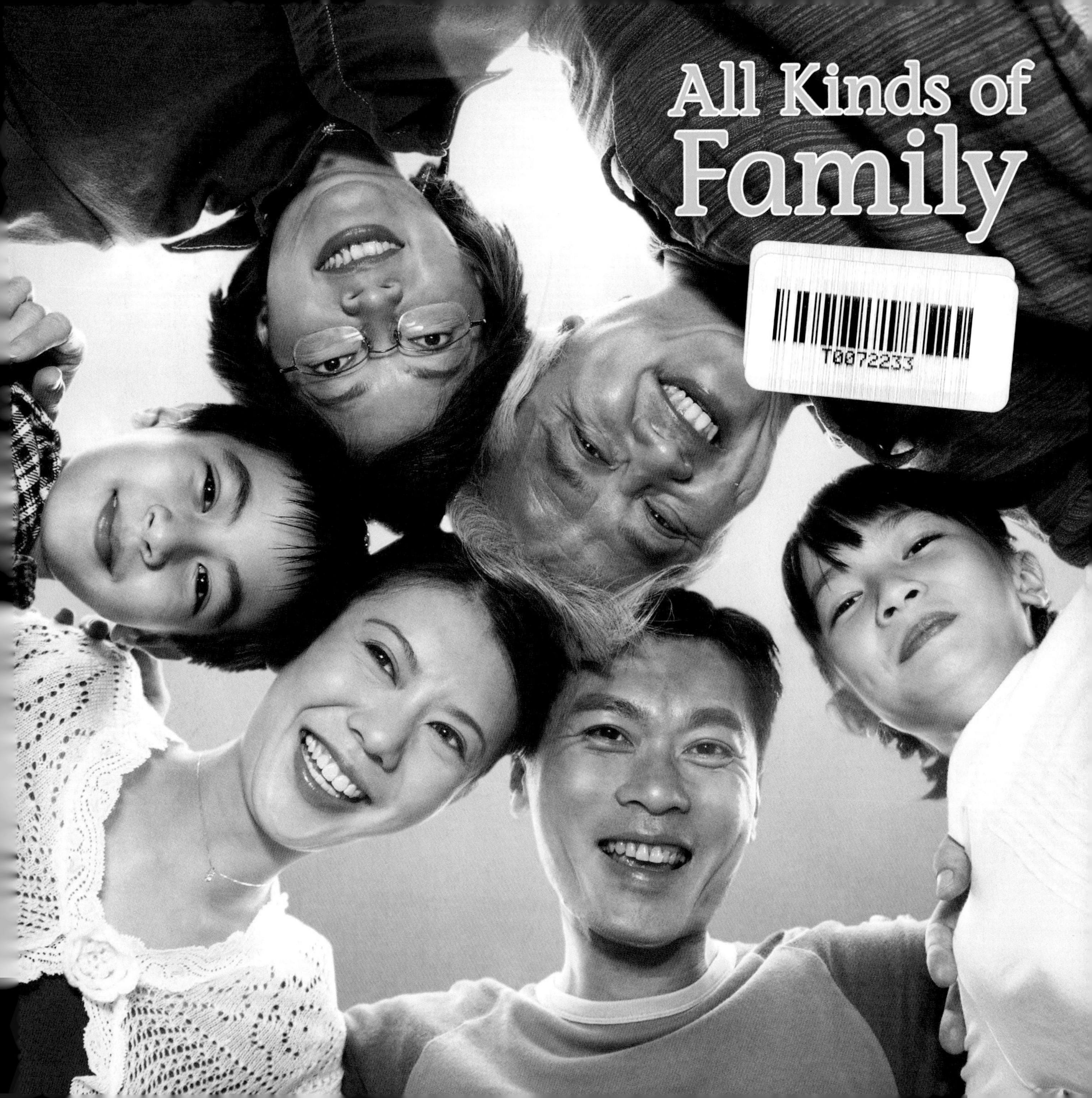

# family

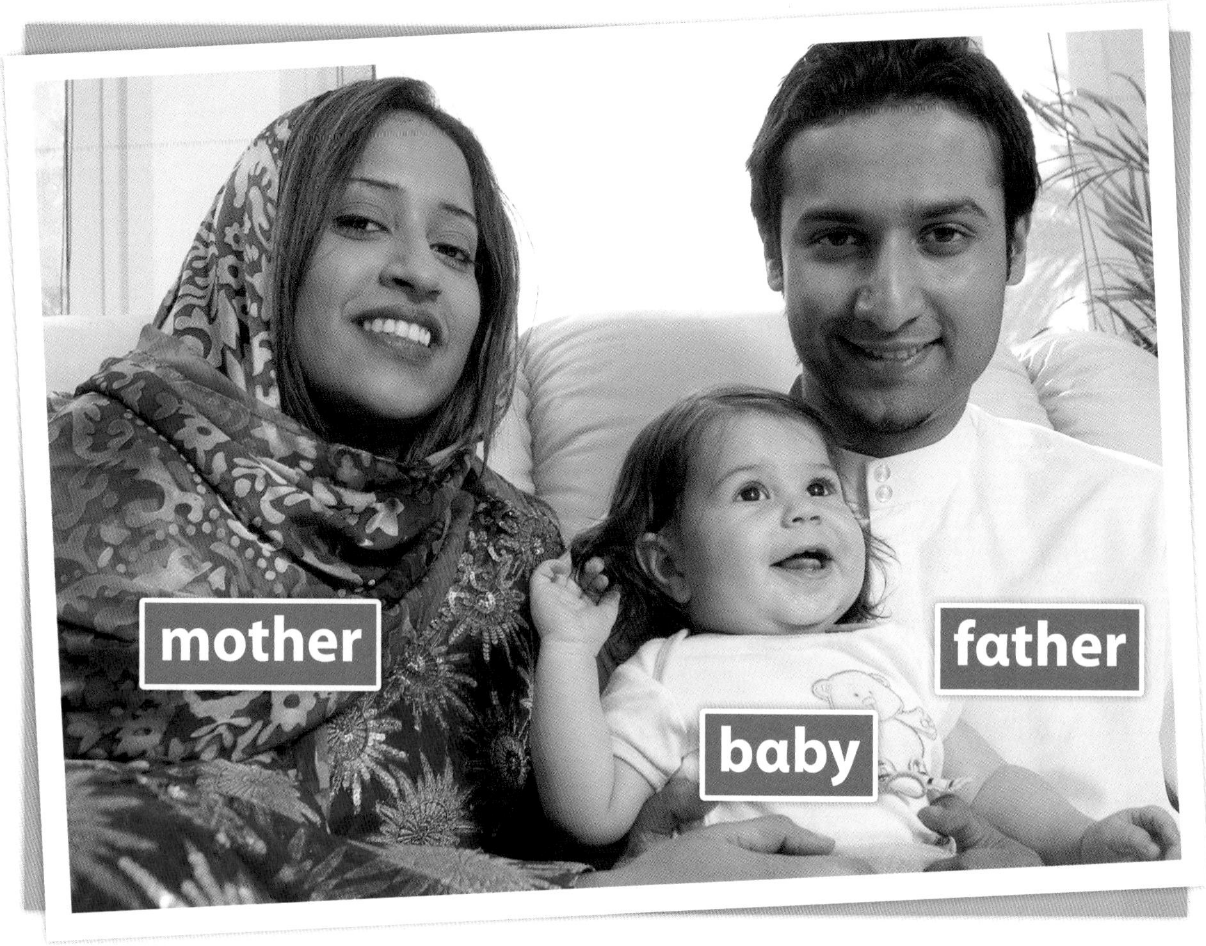

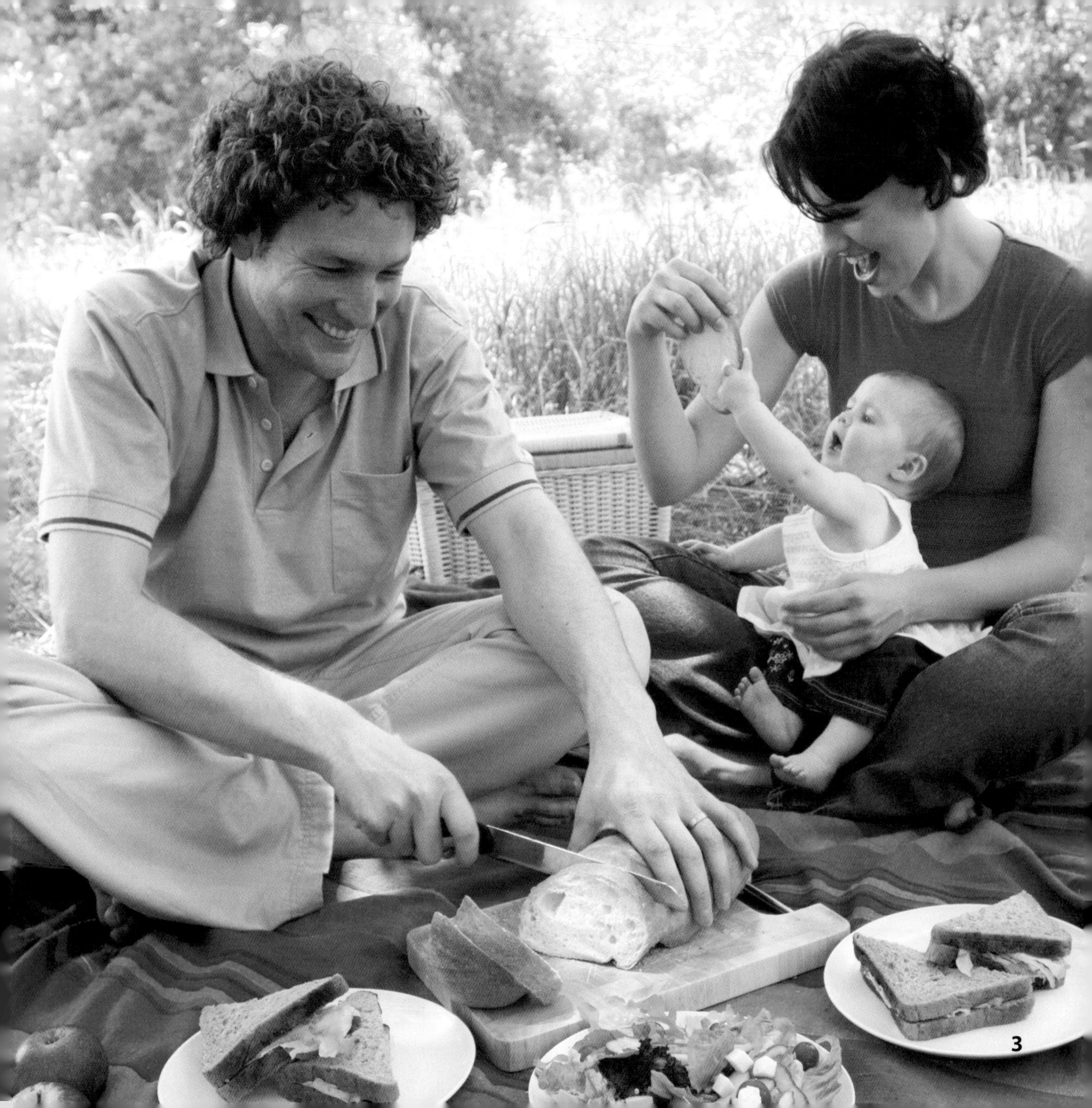

# brothers

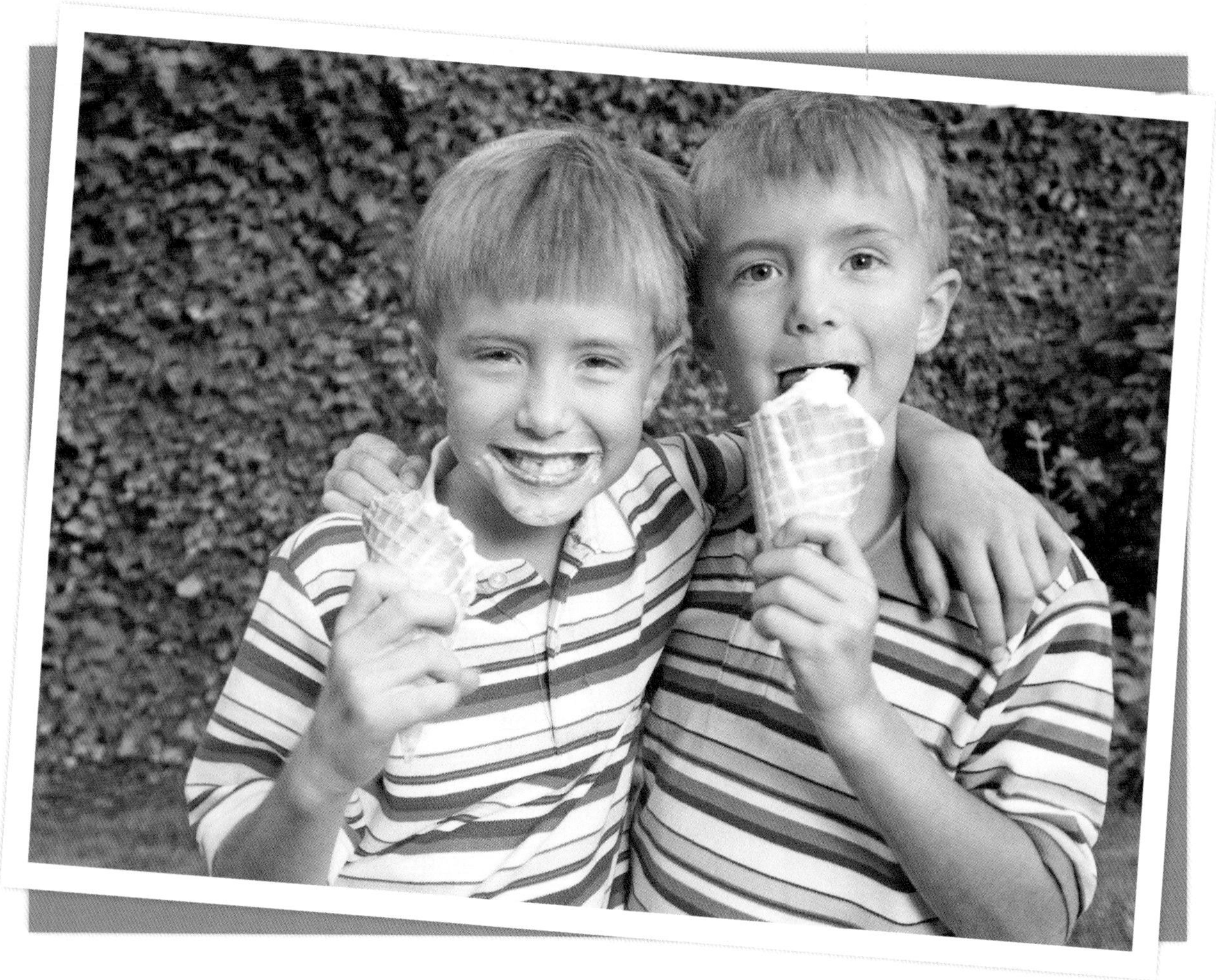

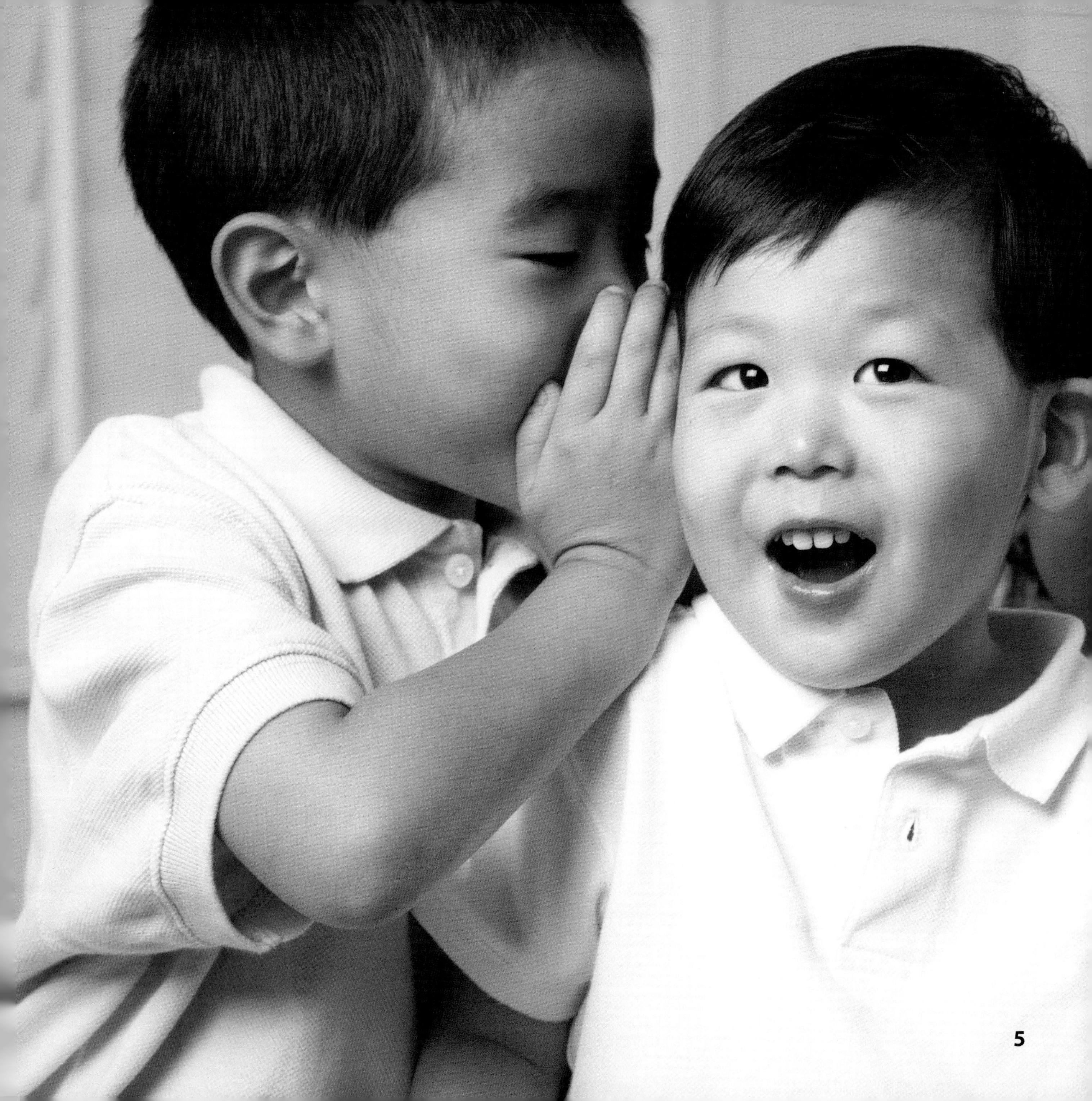

# sisters

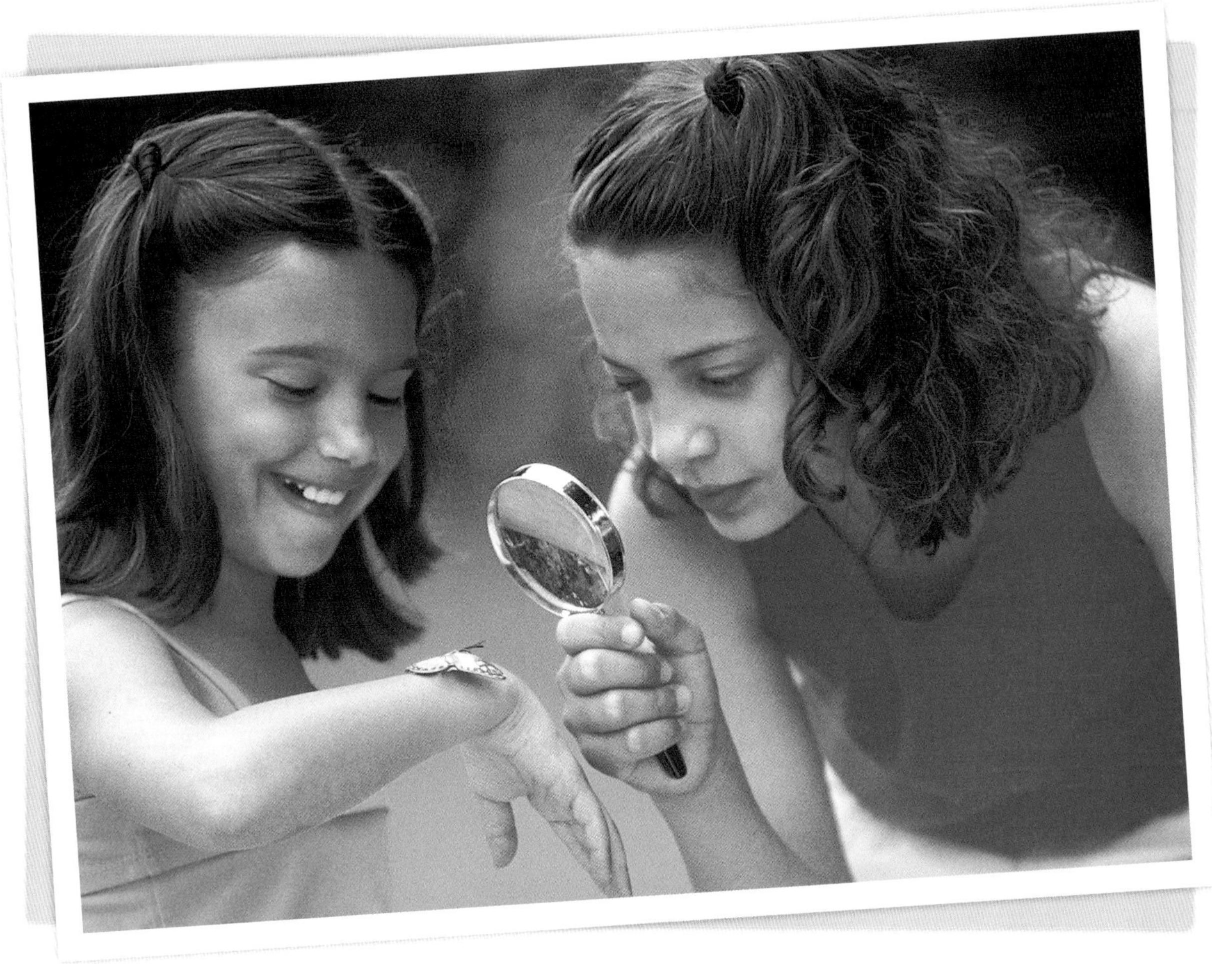

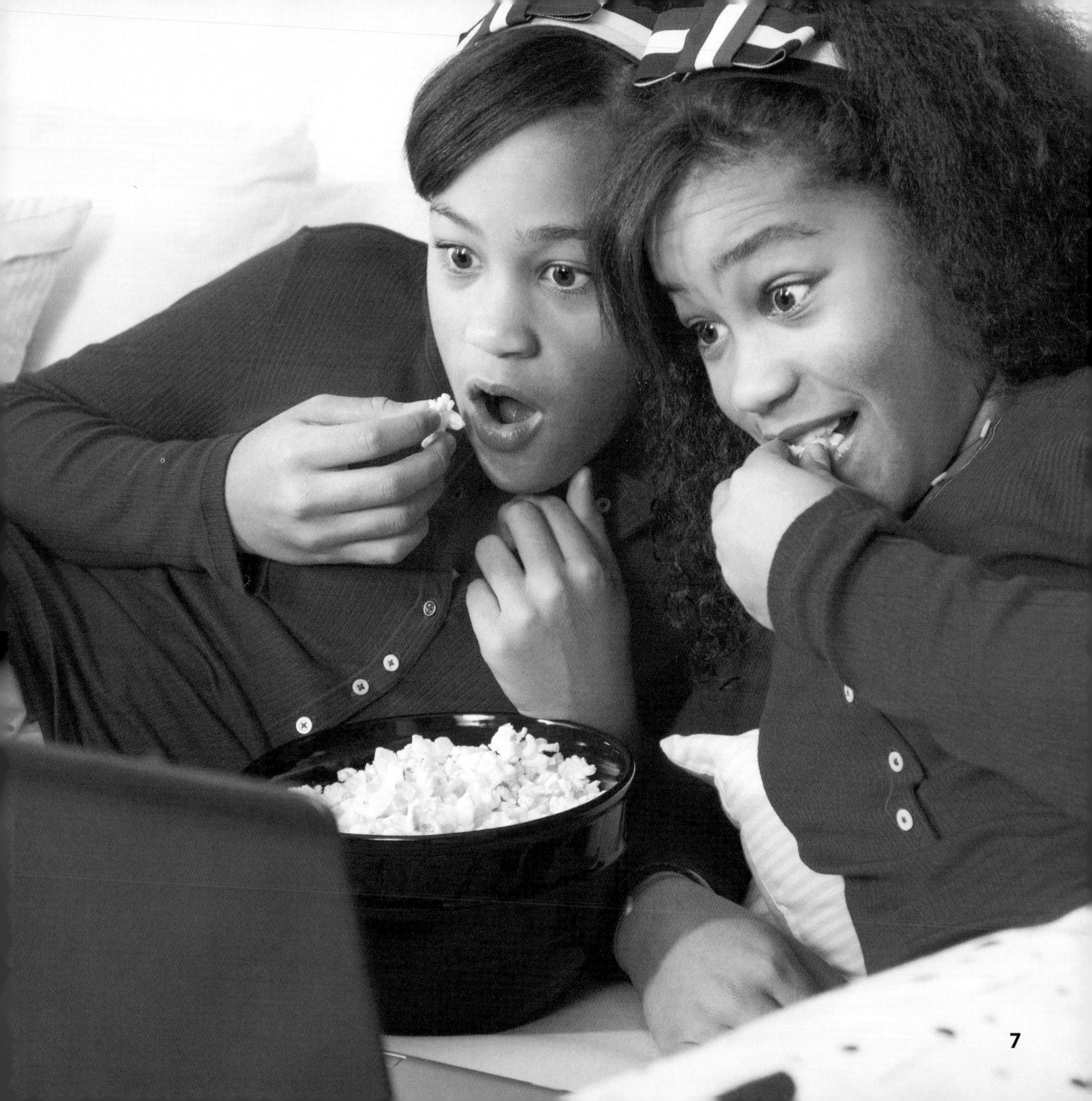

# family

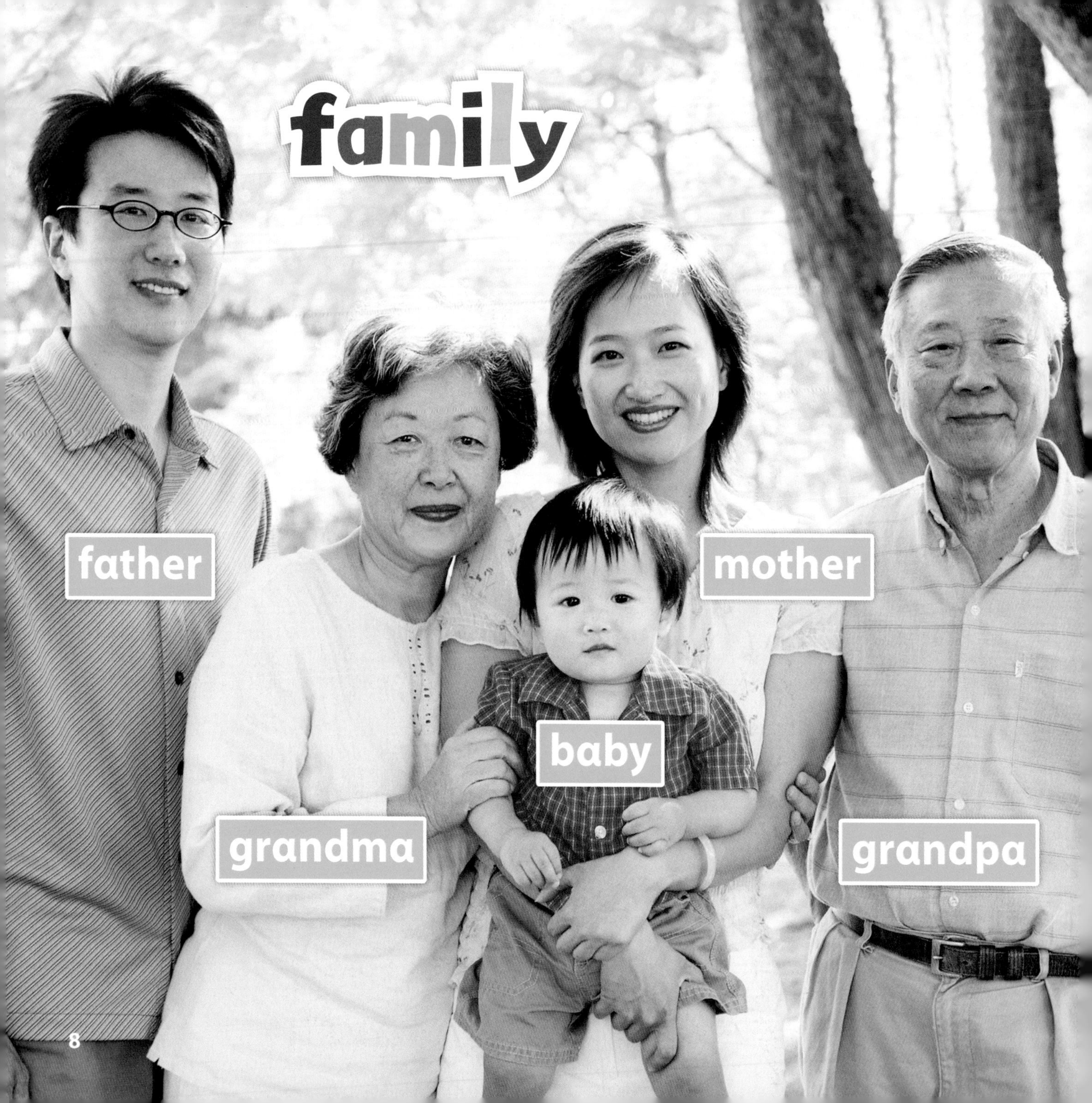